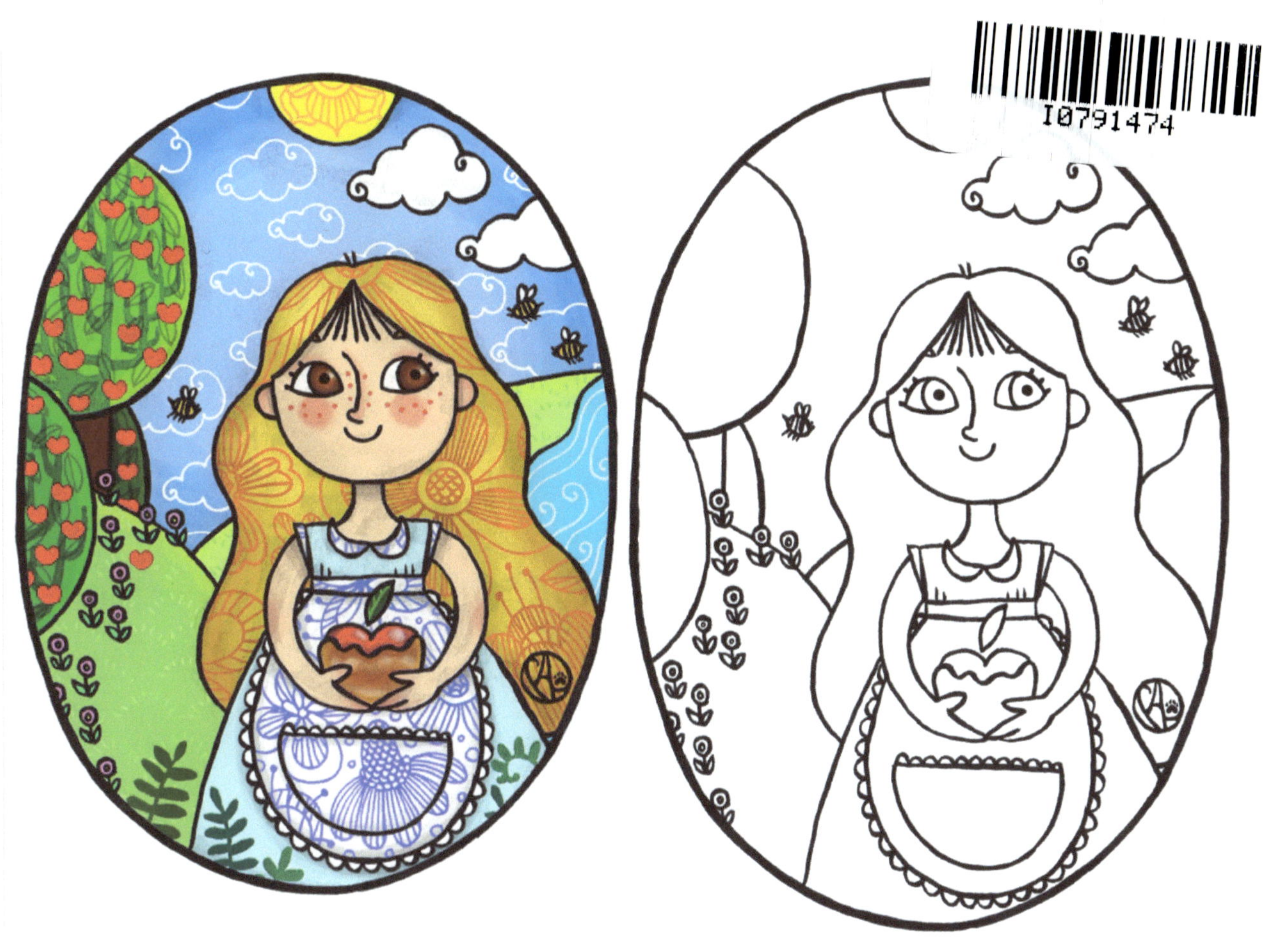

Look at the colored image. Now color the other so they look the same.

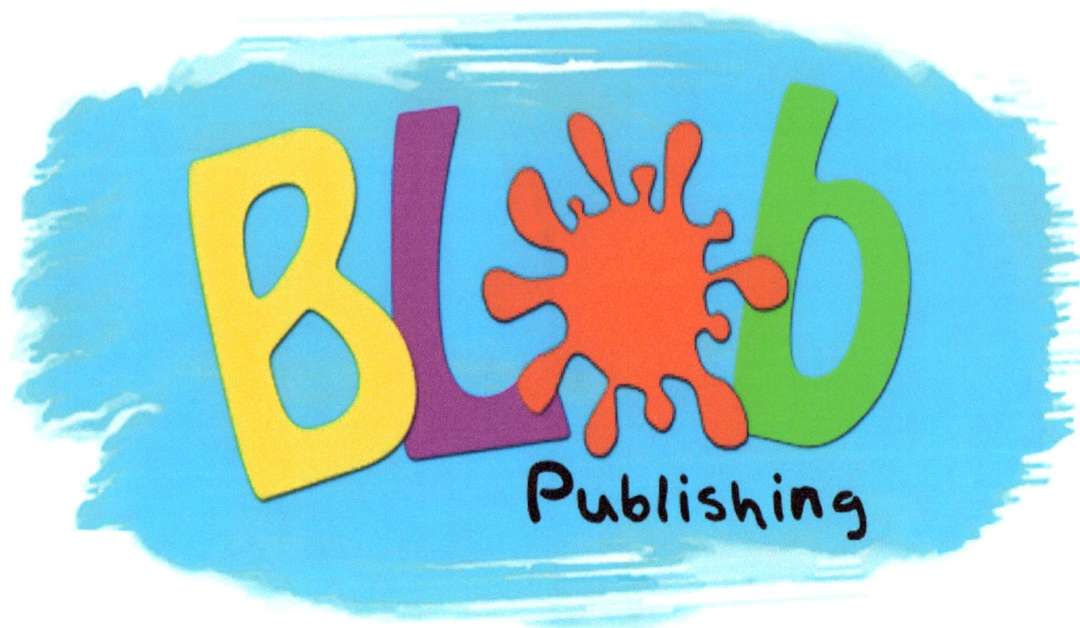

BLOb
Publishing

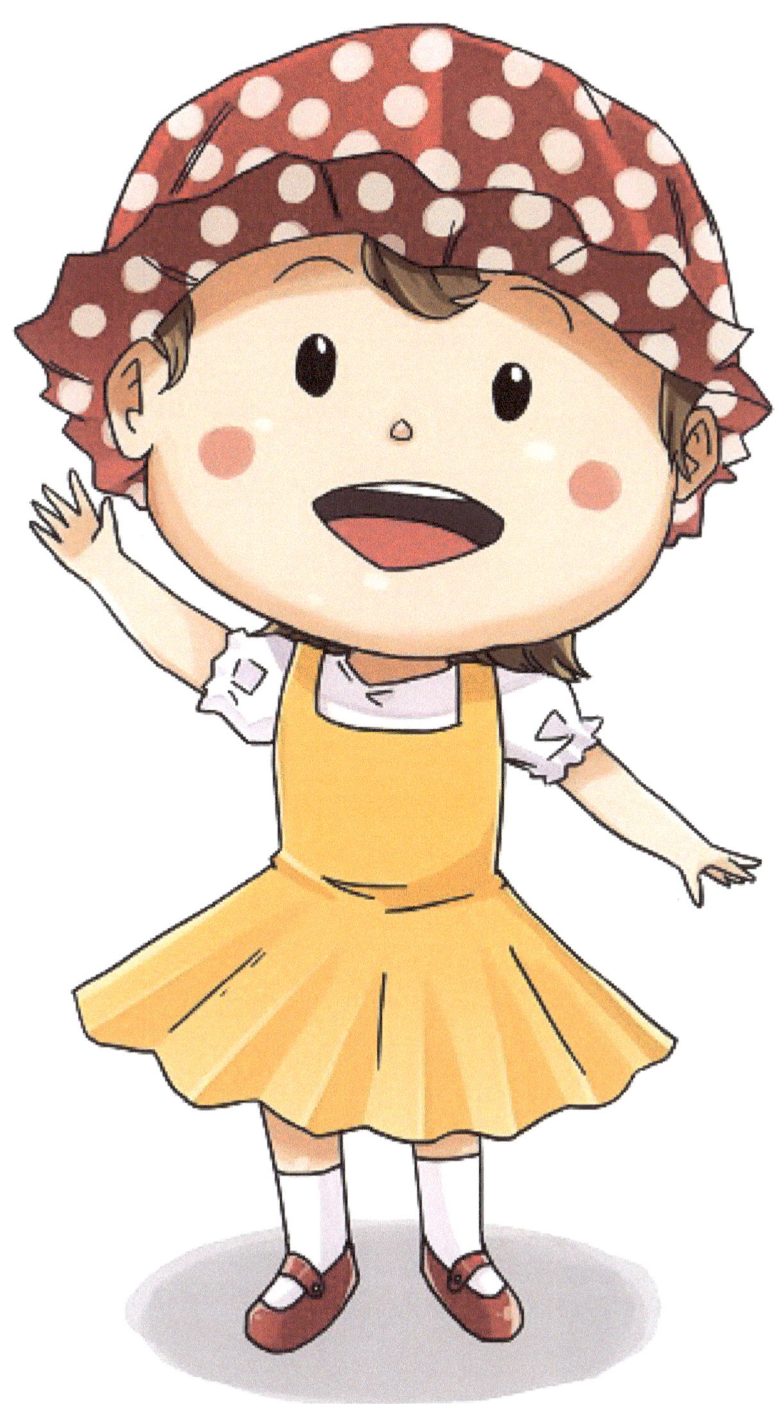

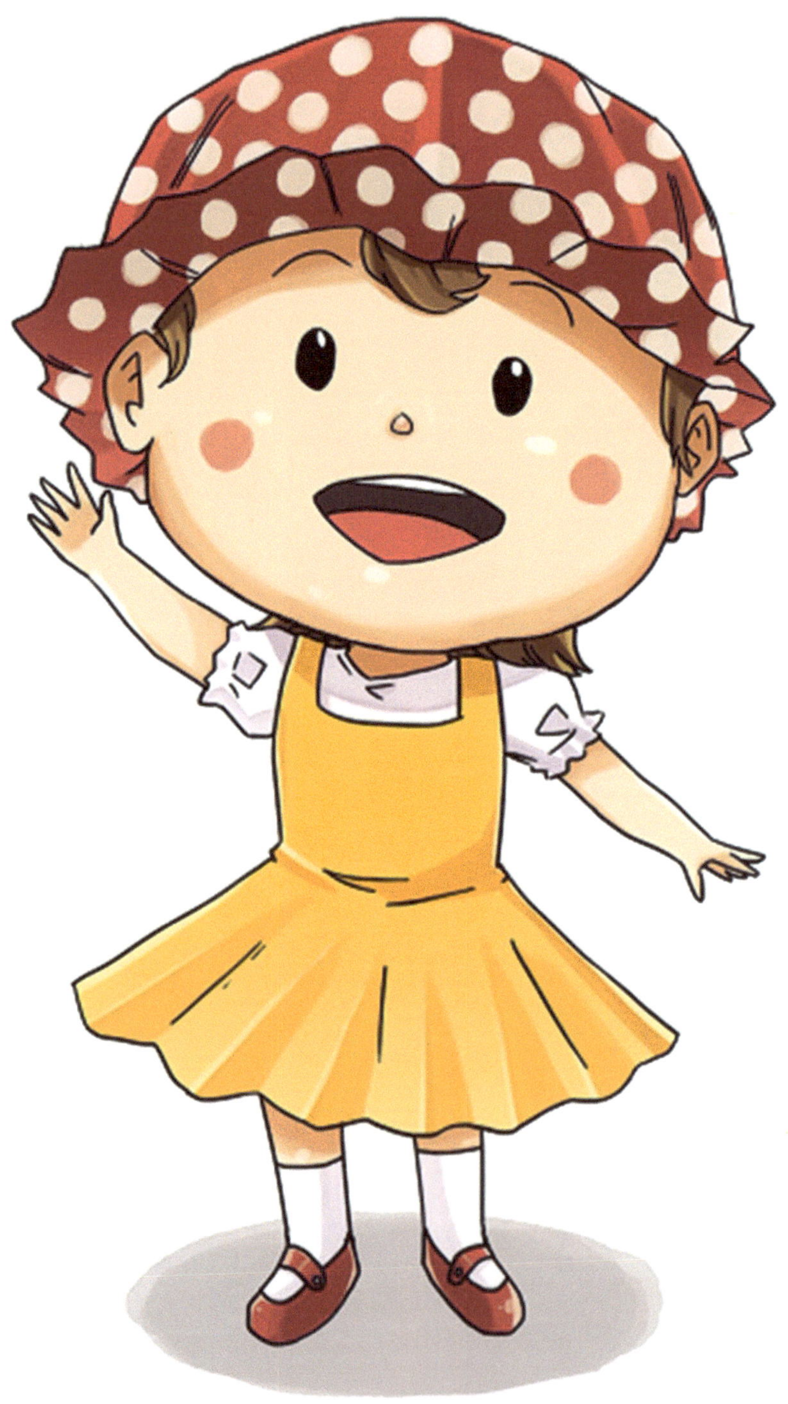

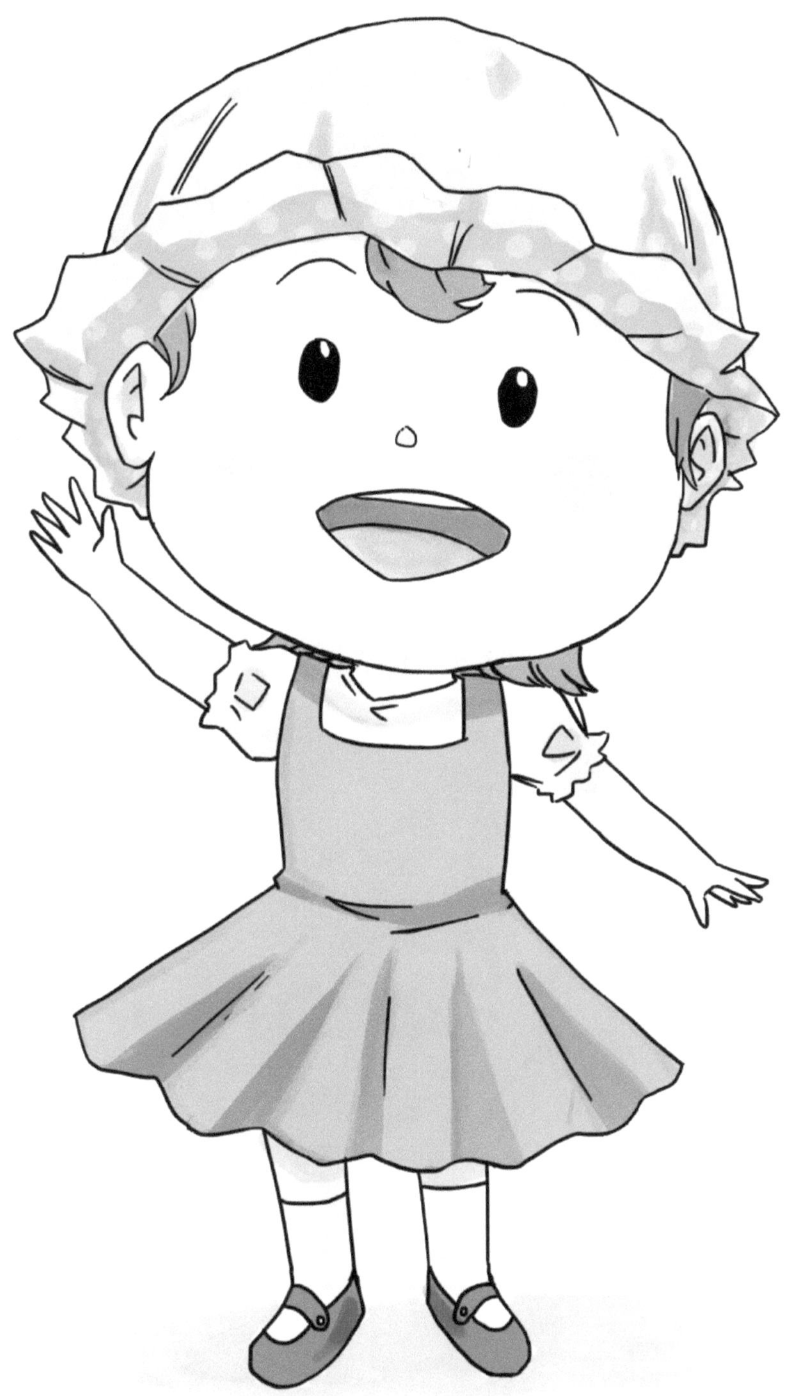

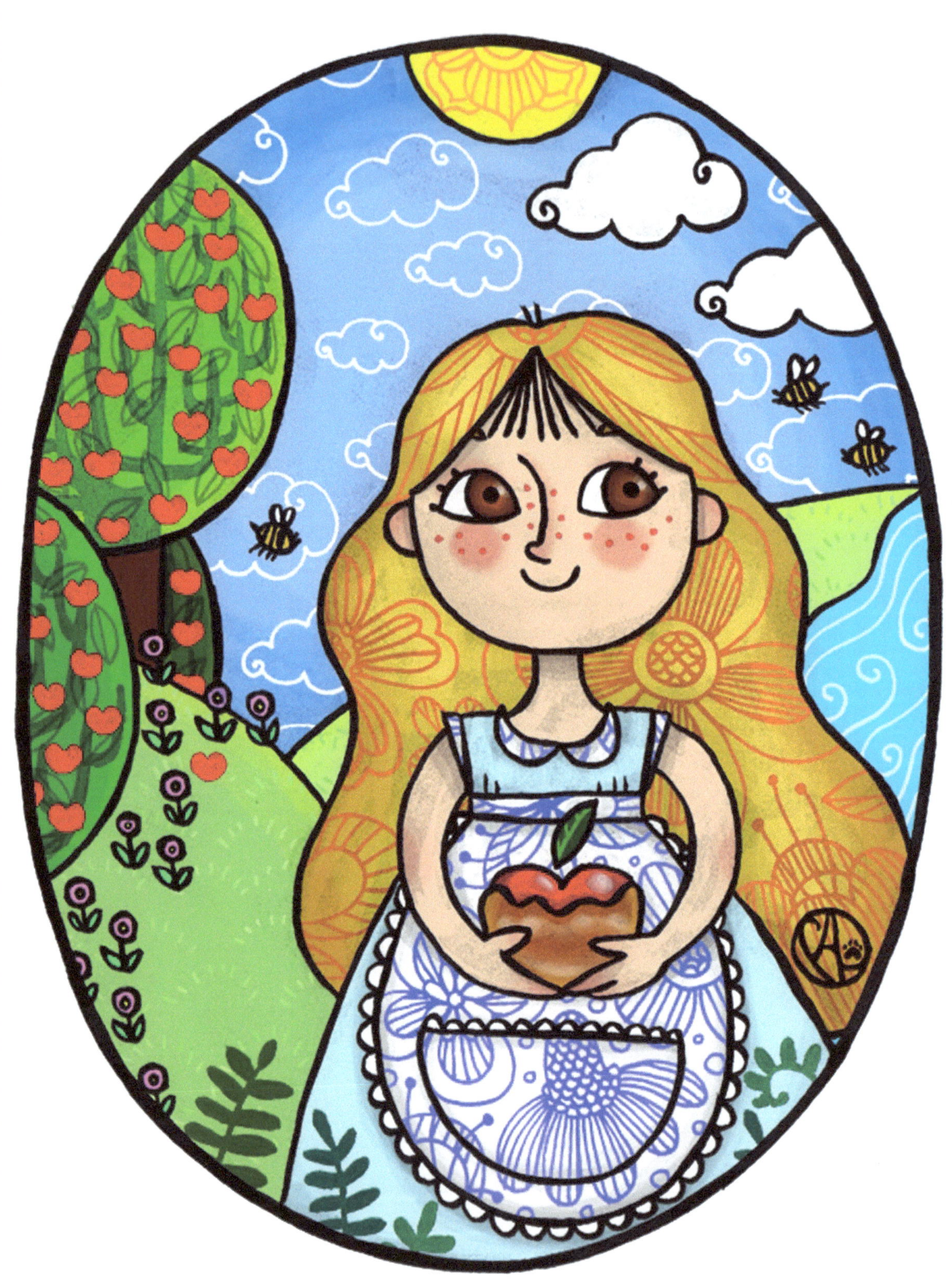

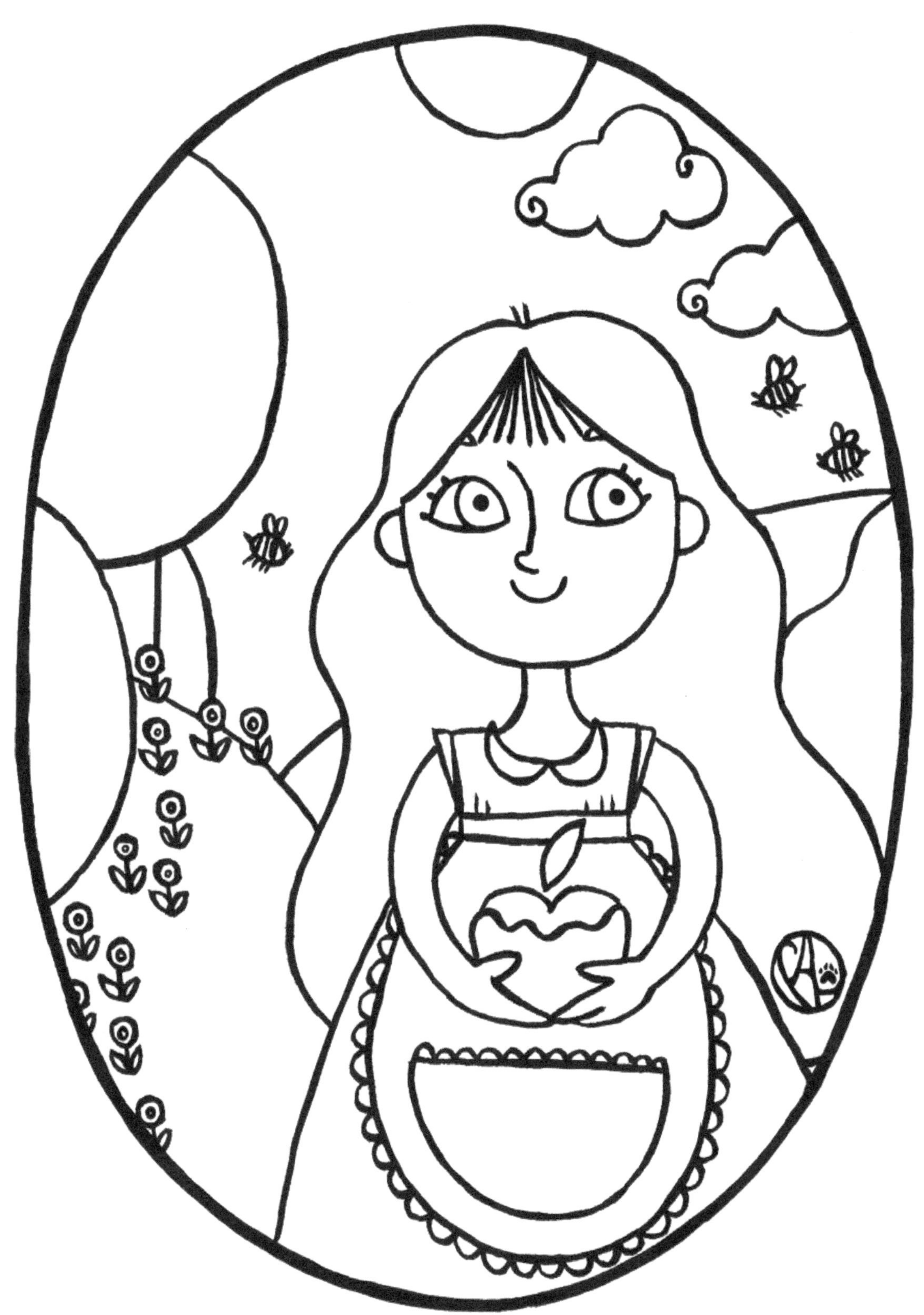

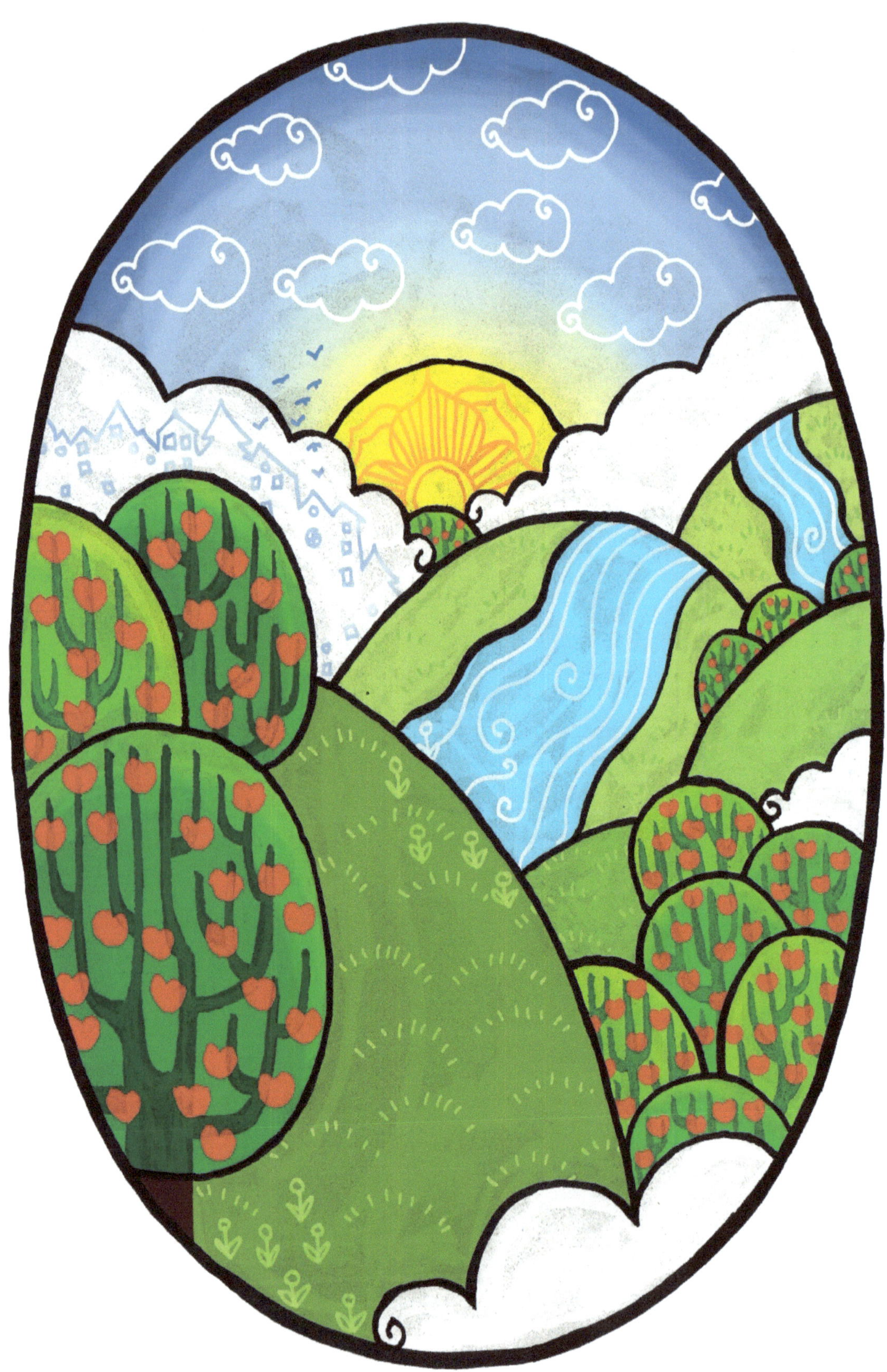

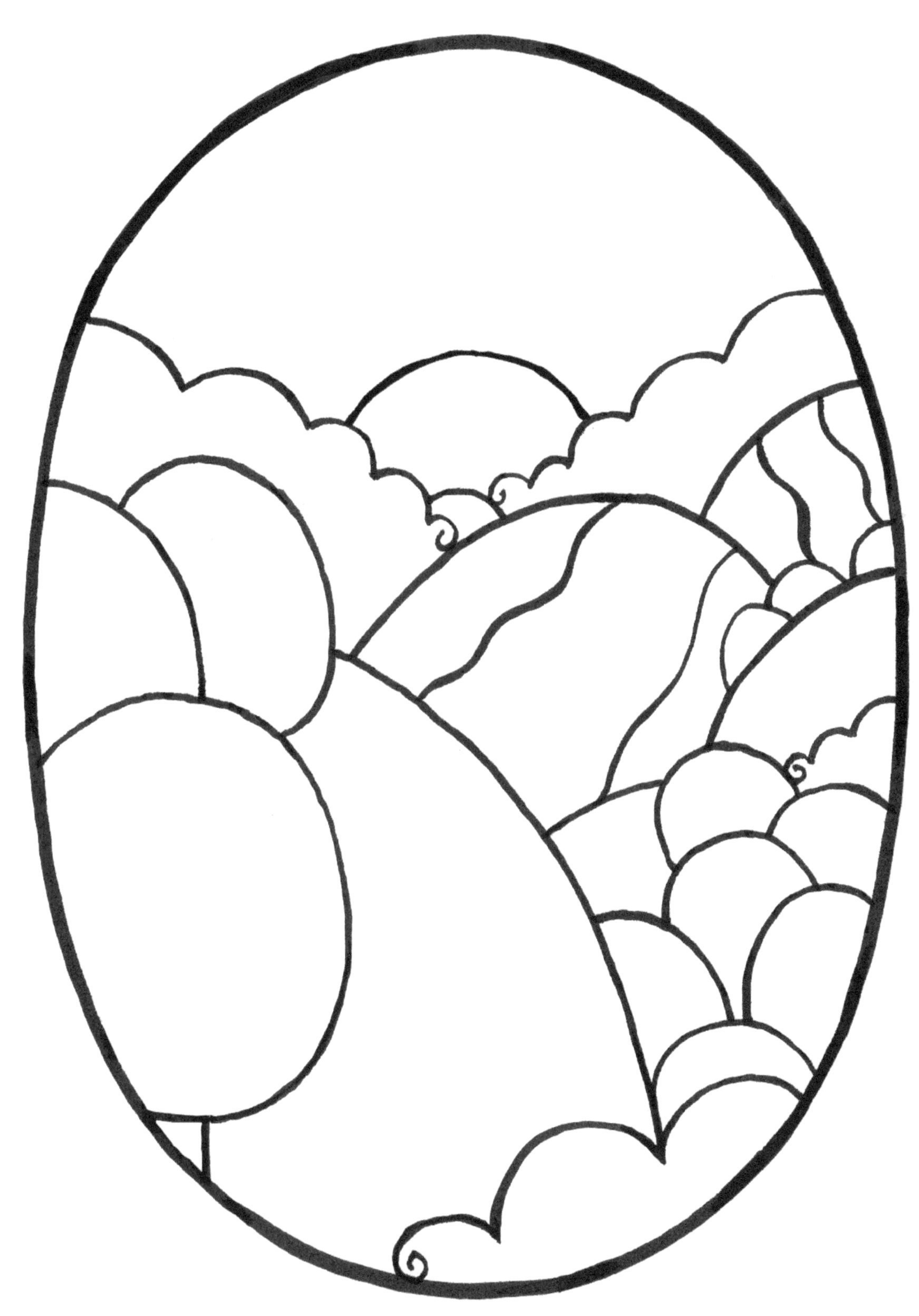

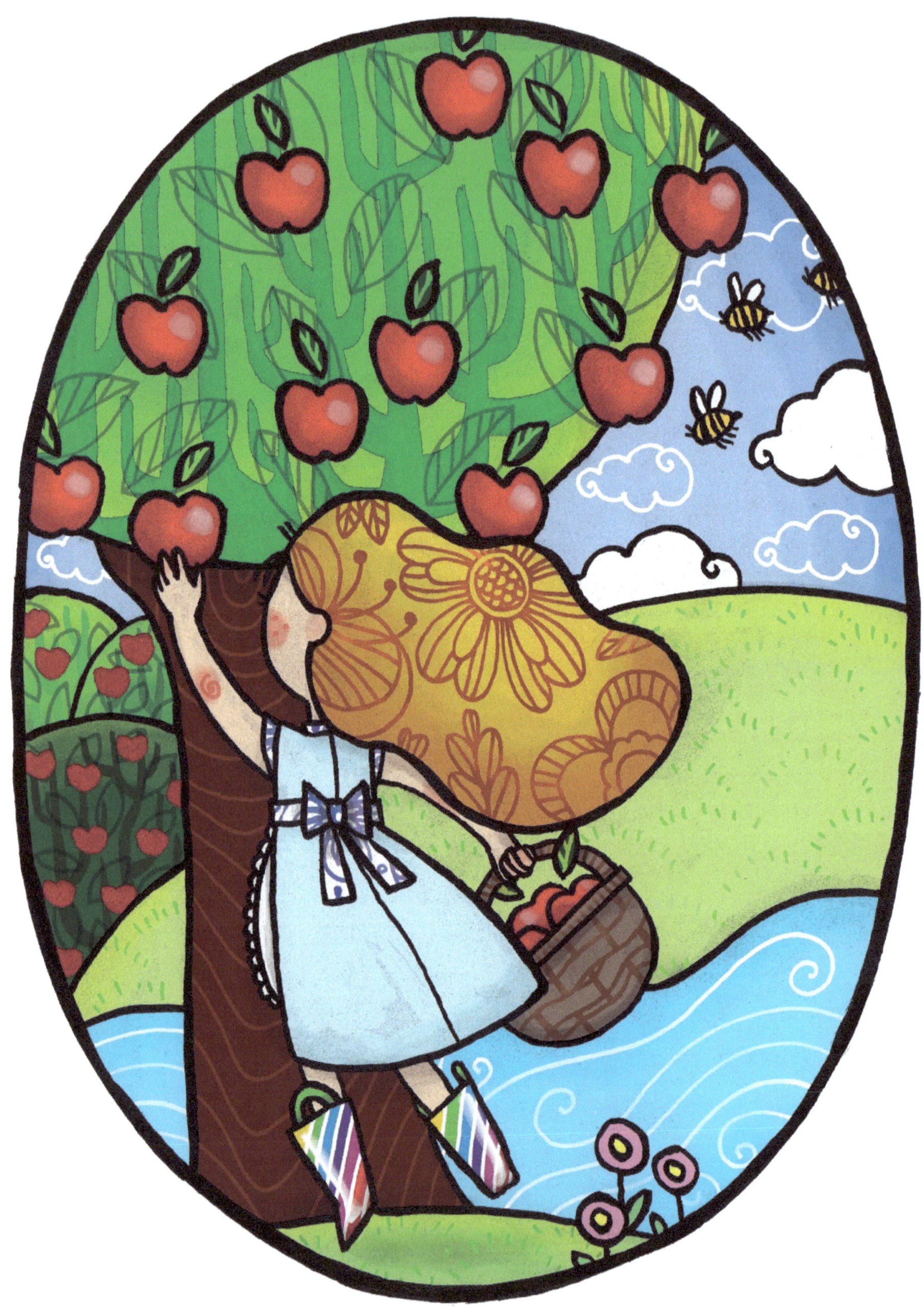

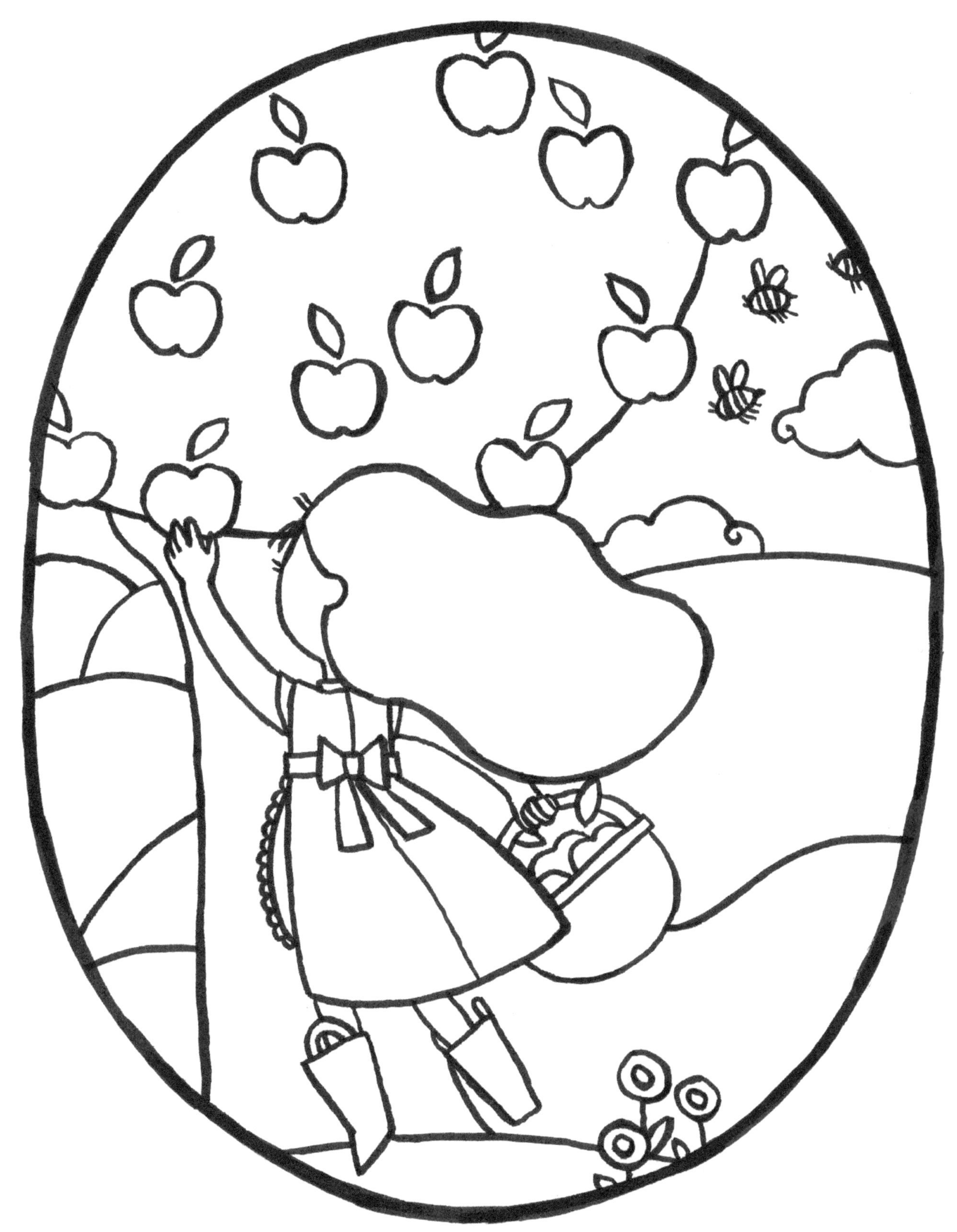

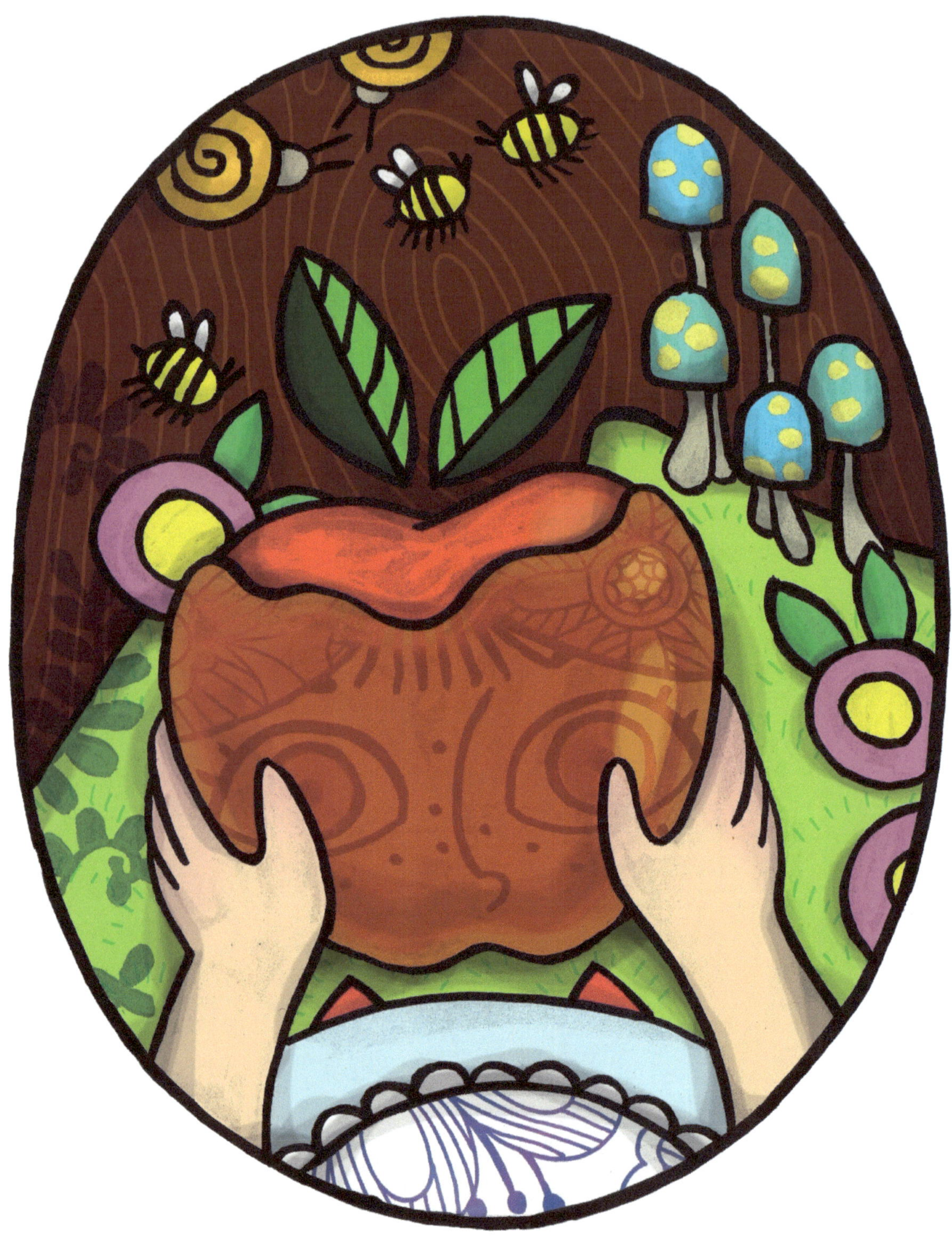

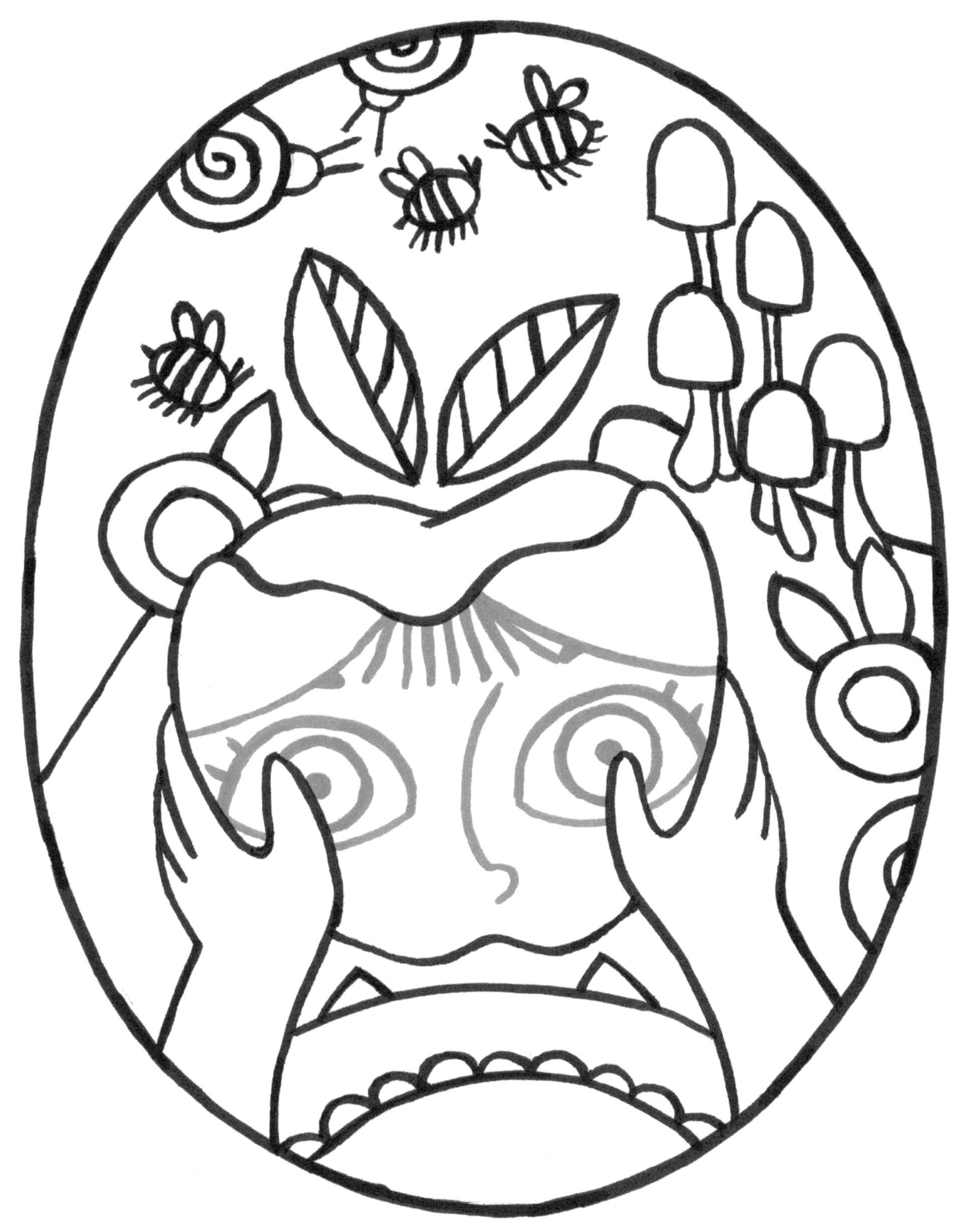

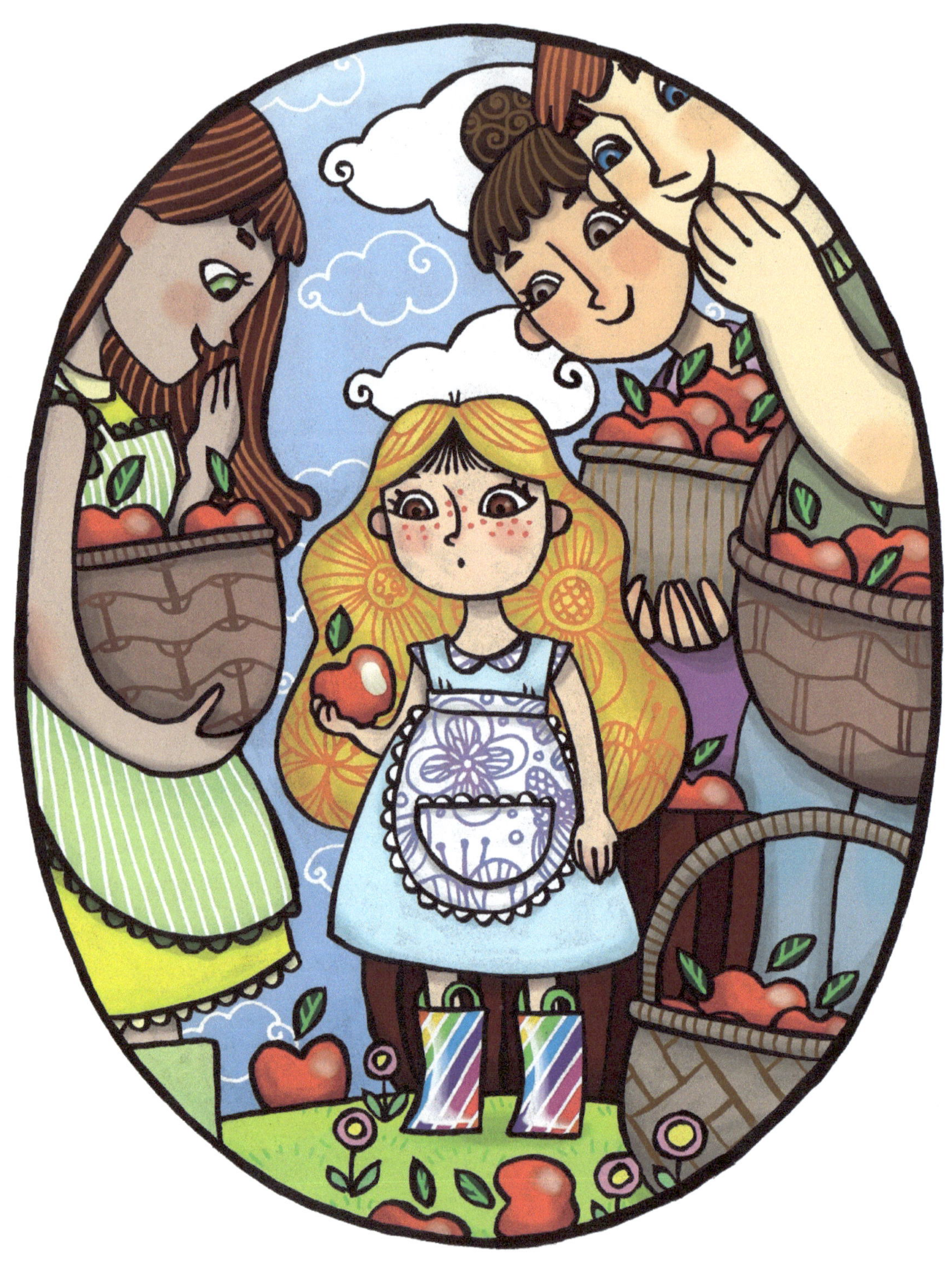

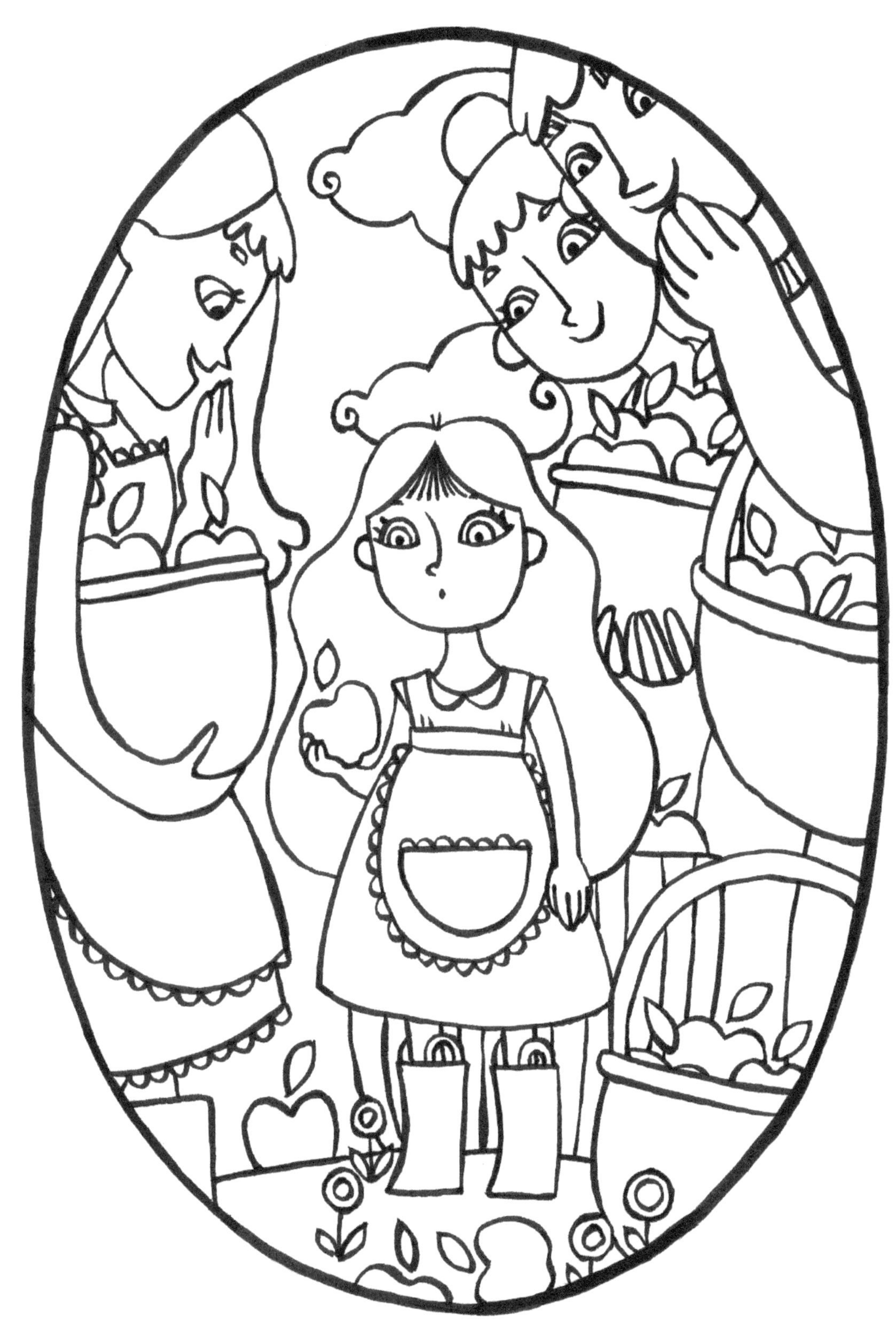

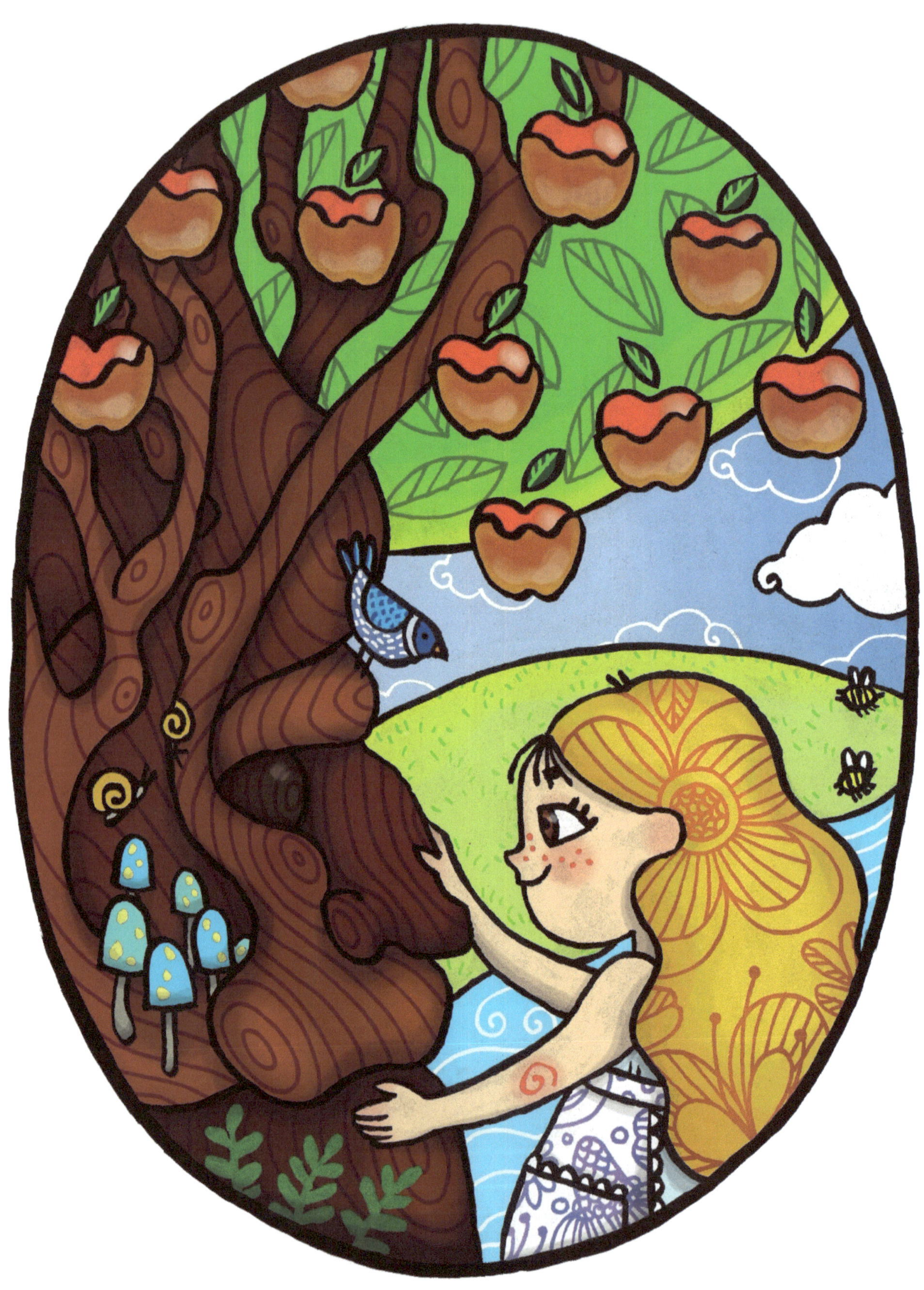

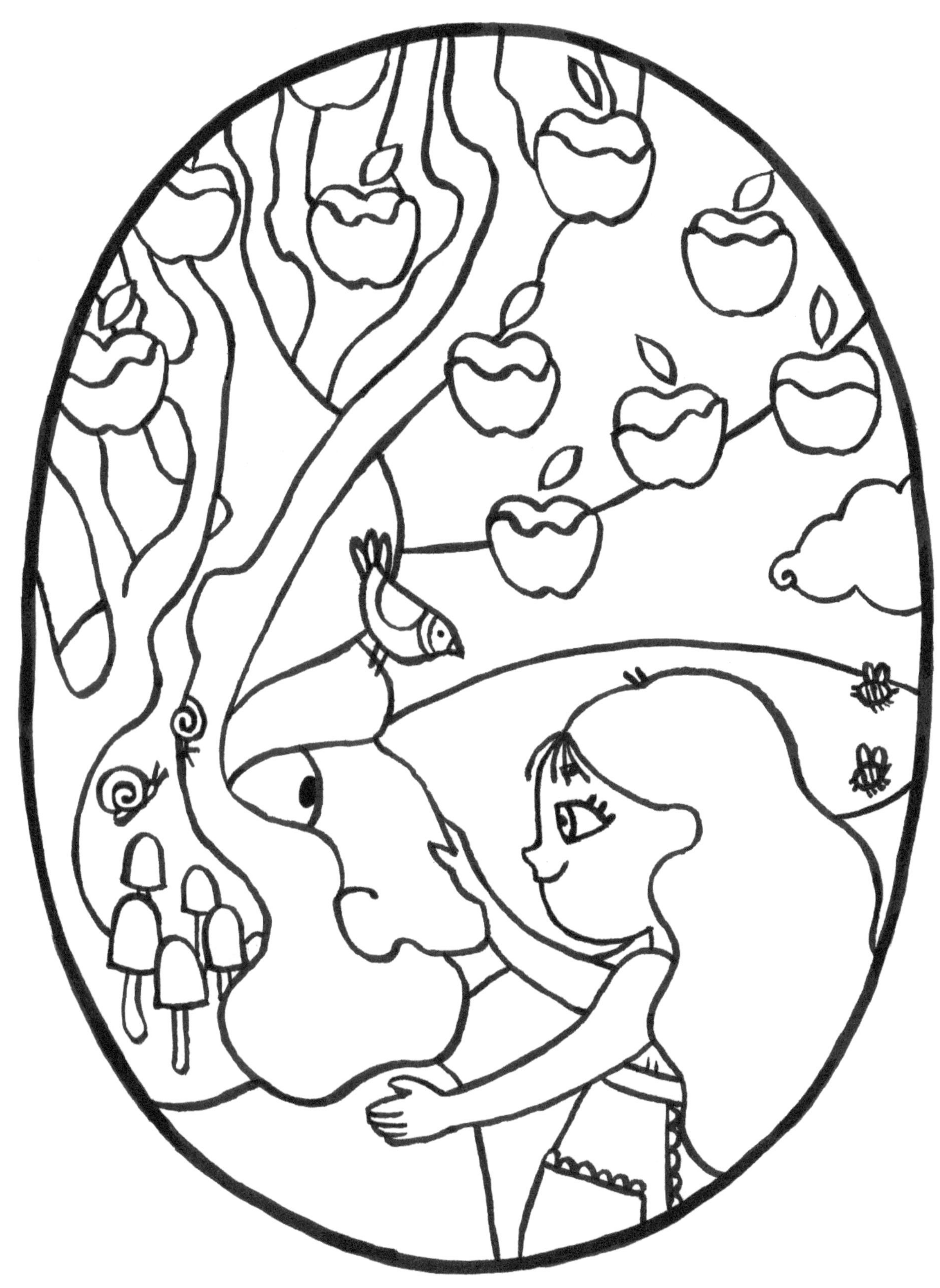

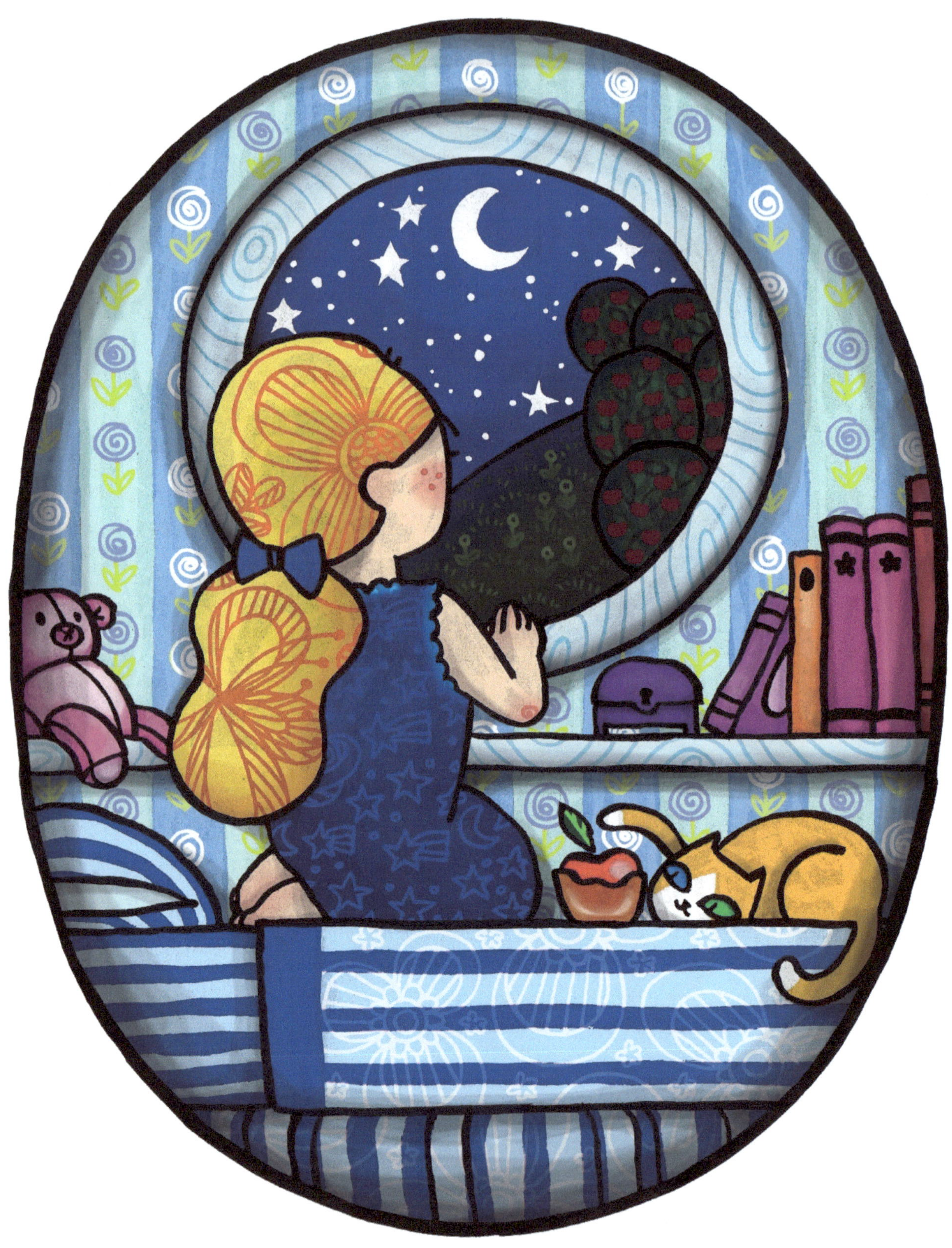

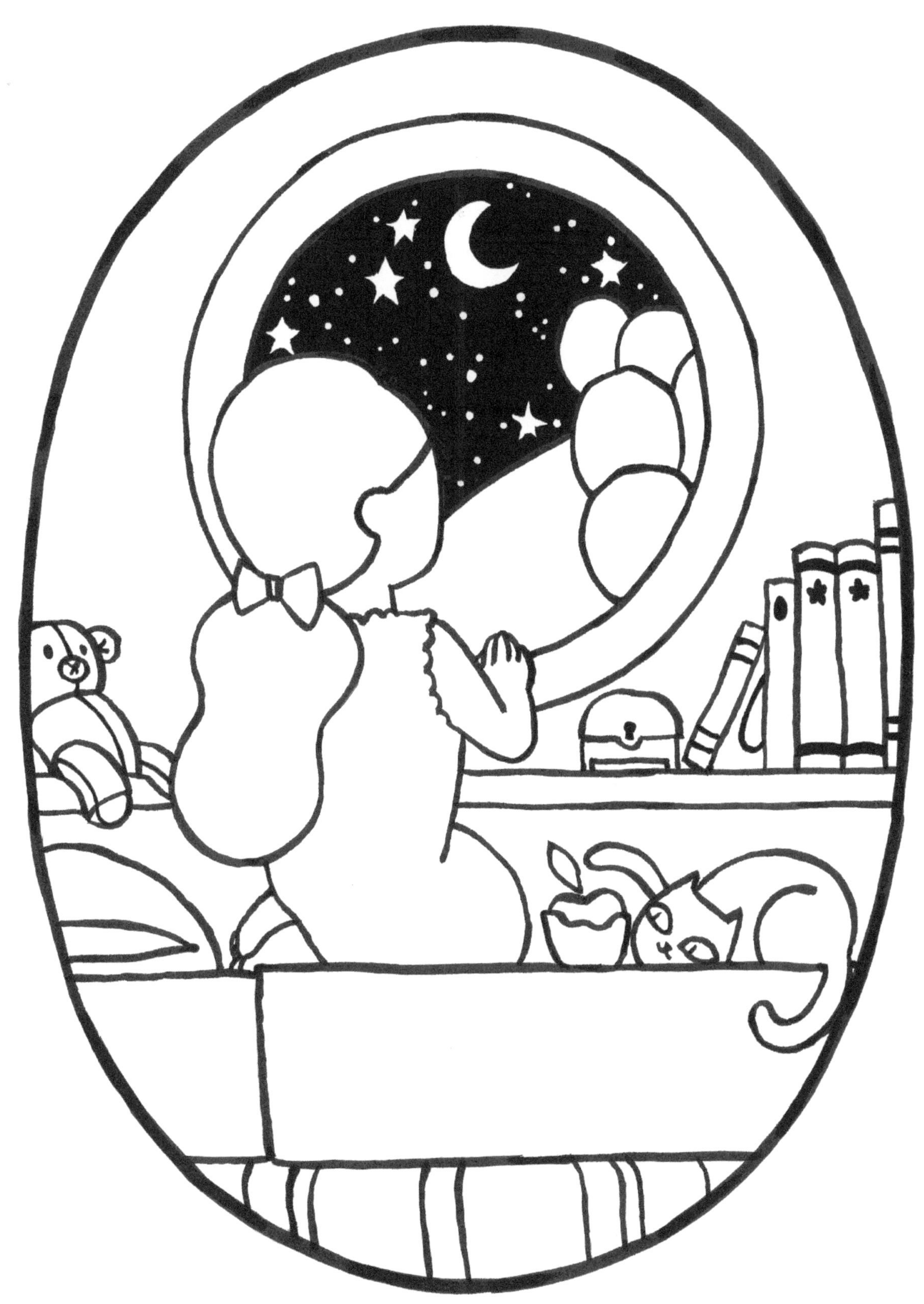

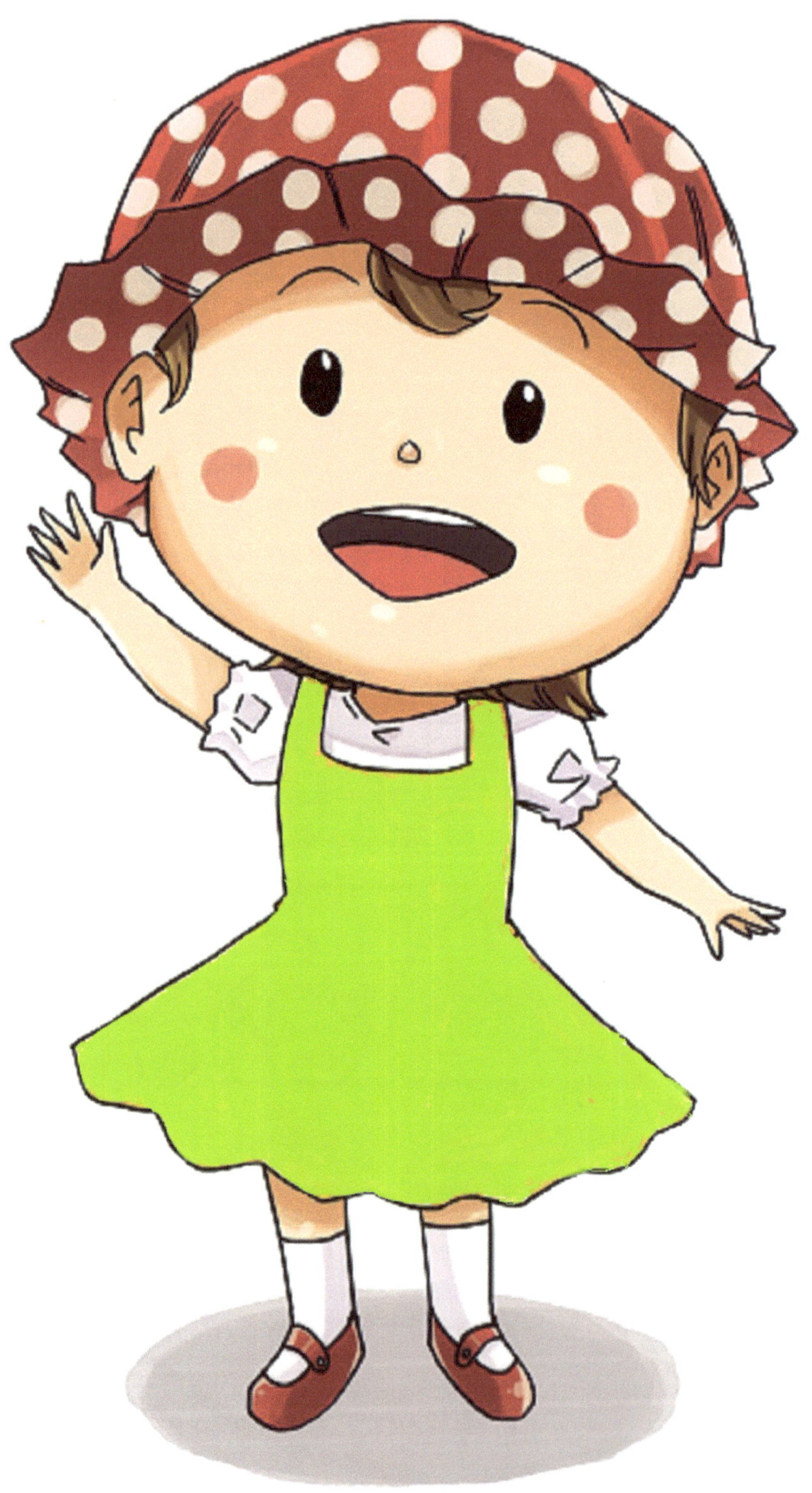

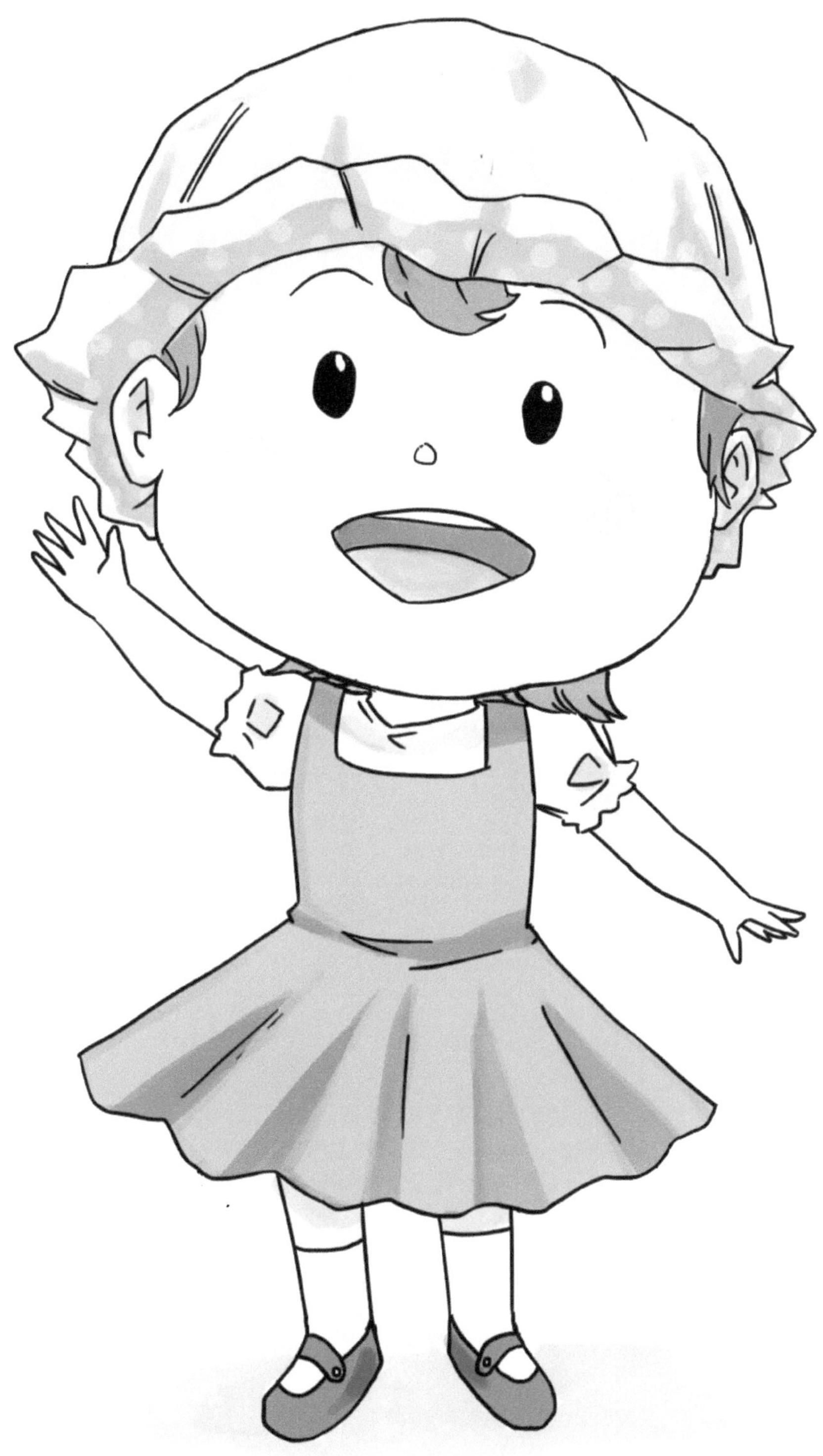

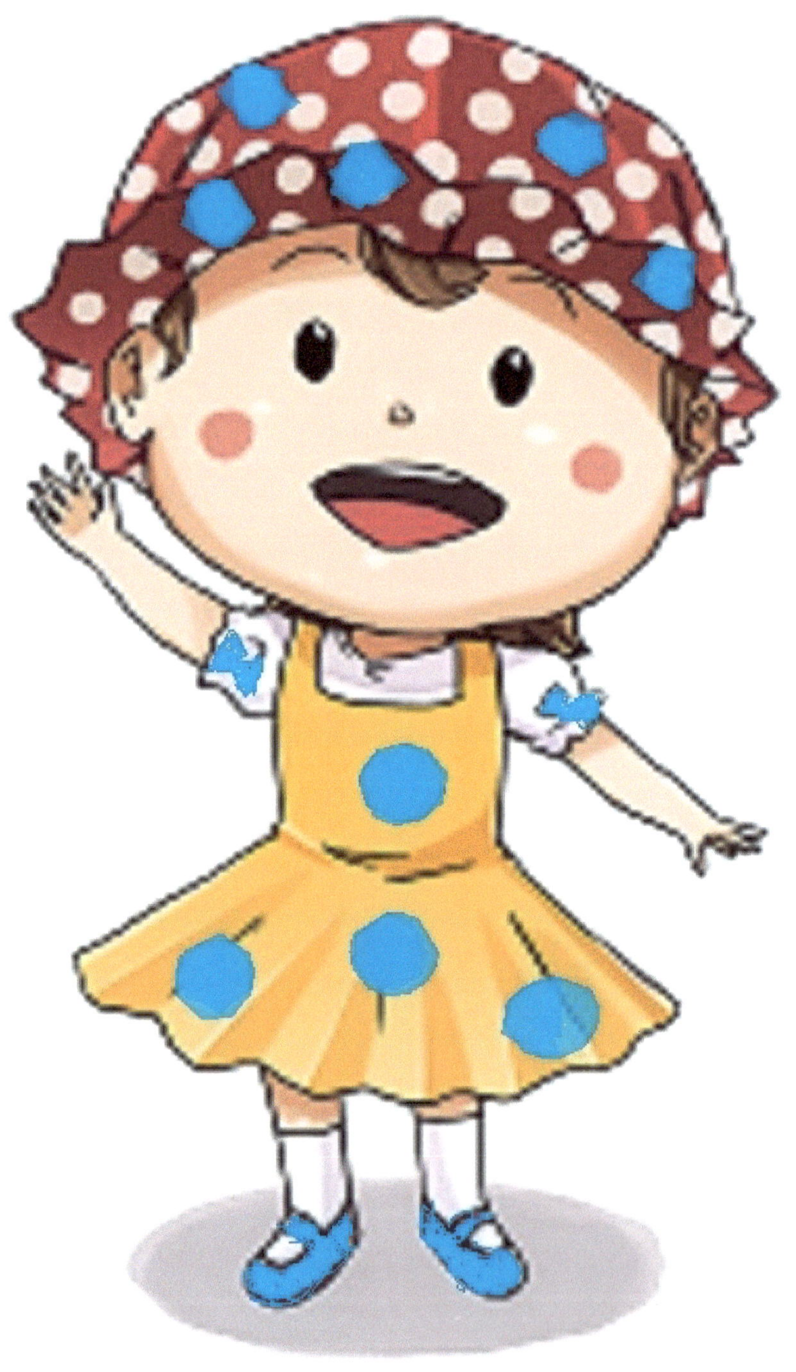

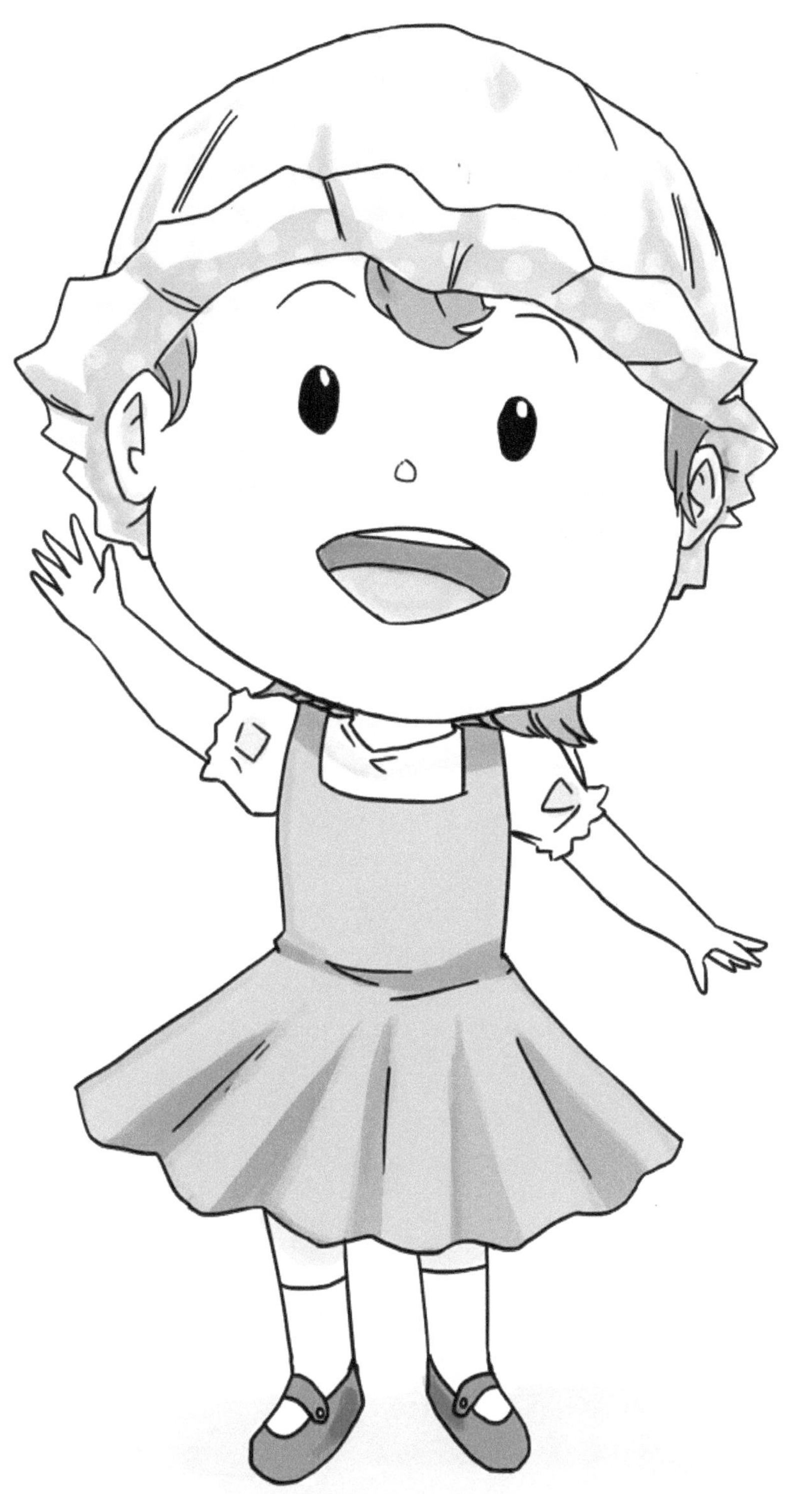

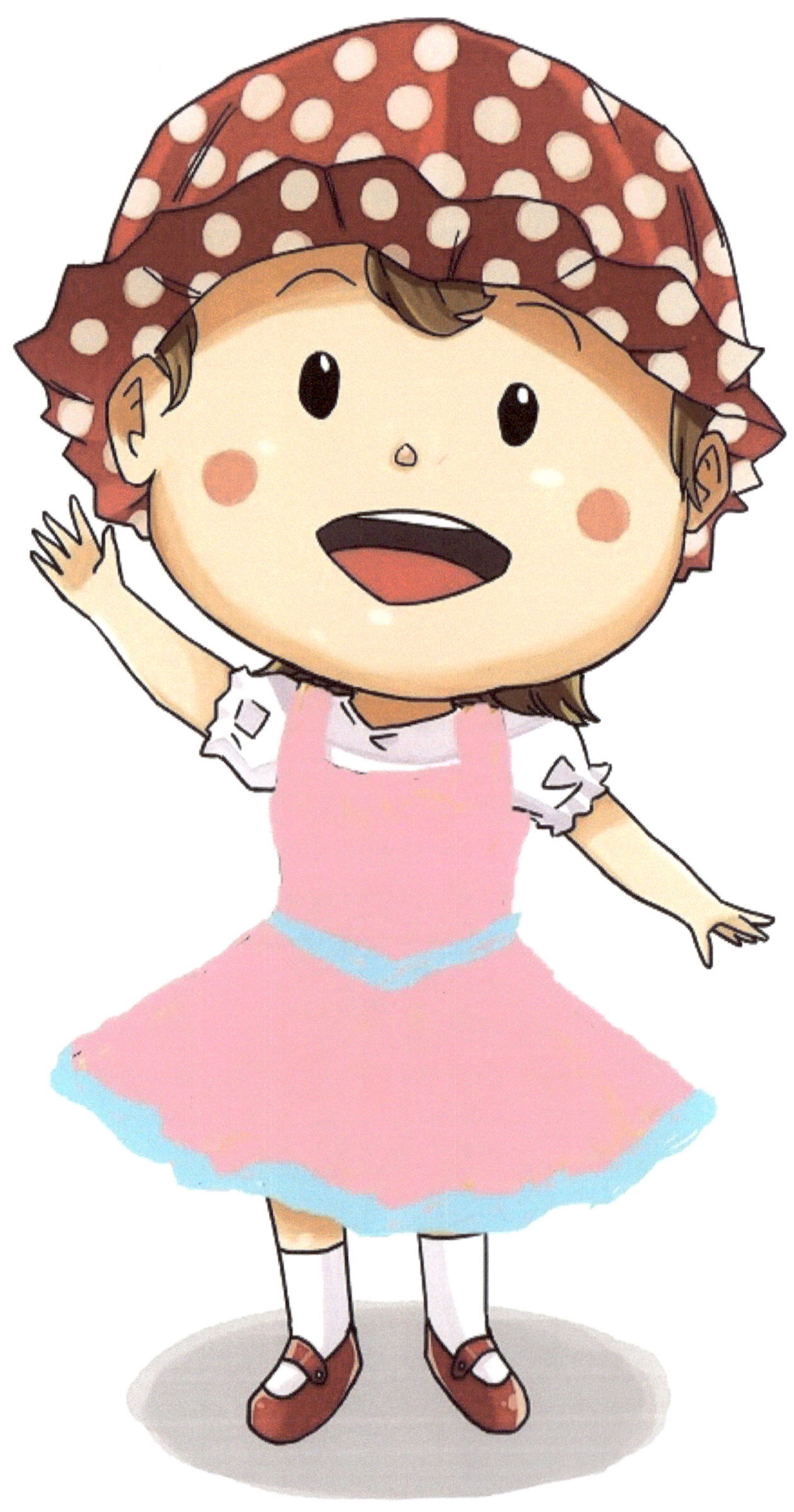

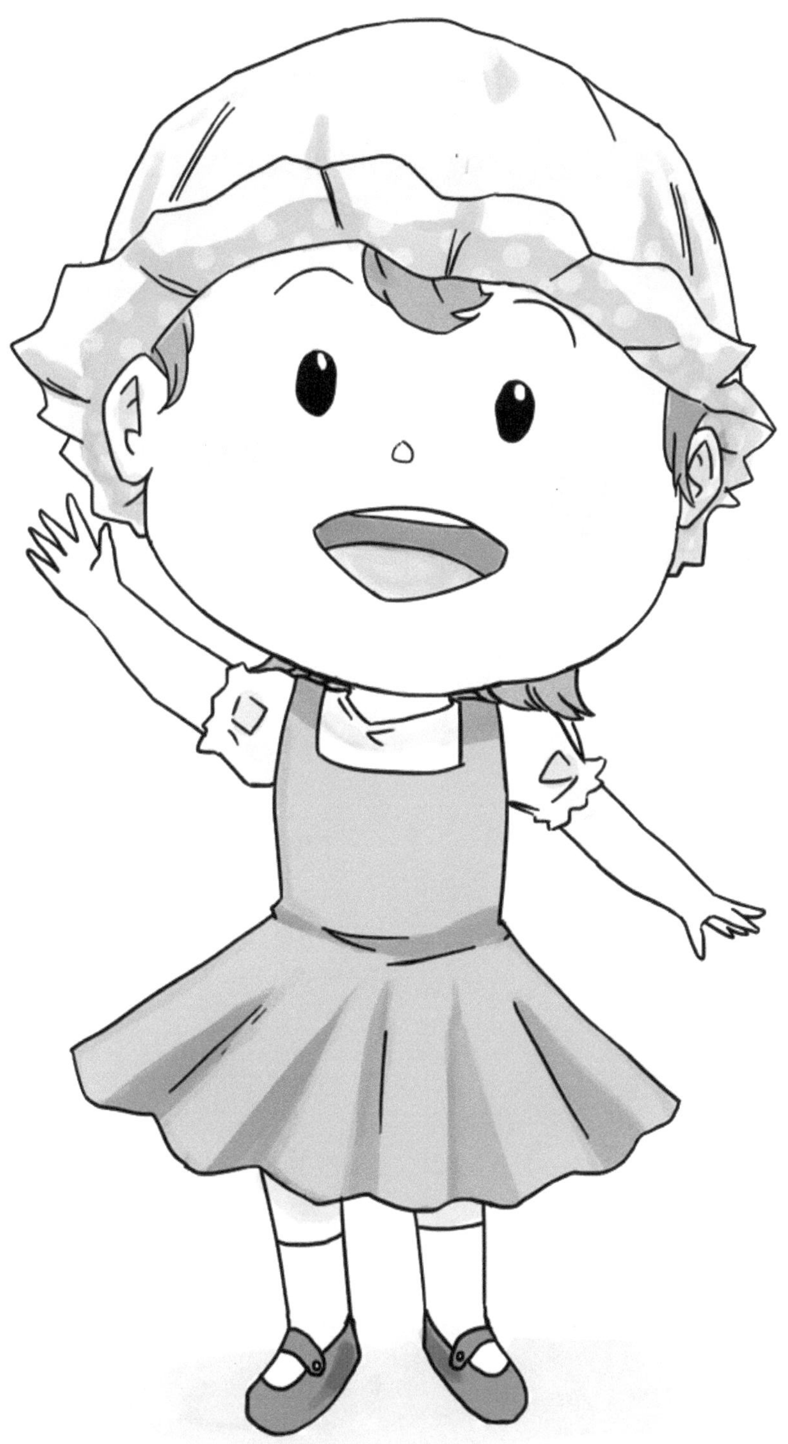

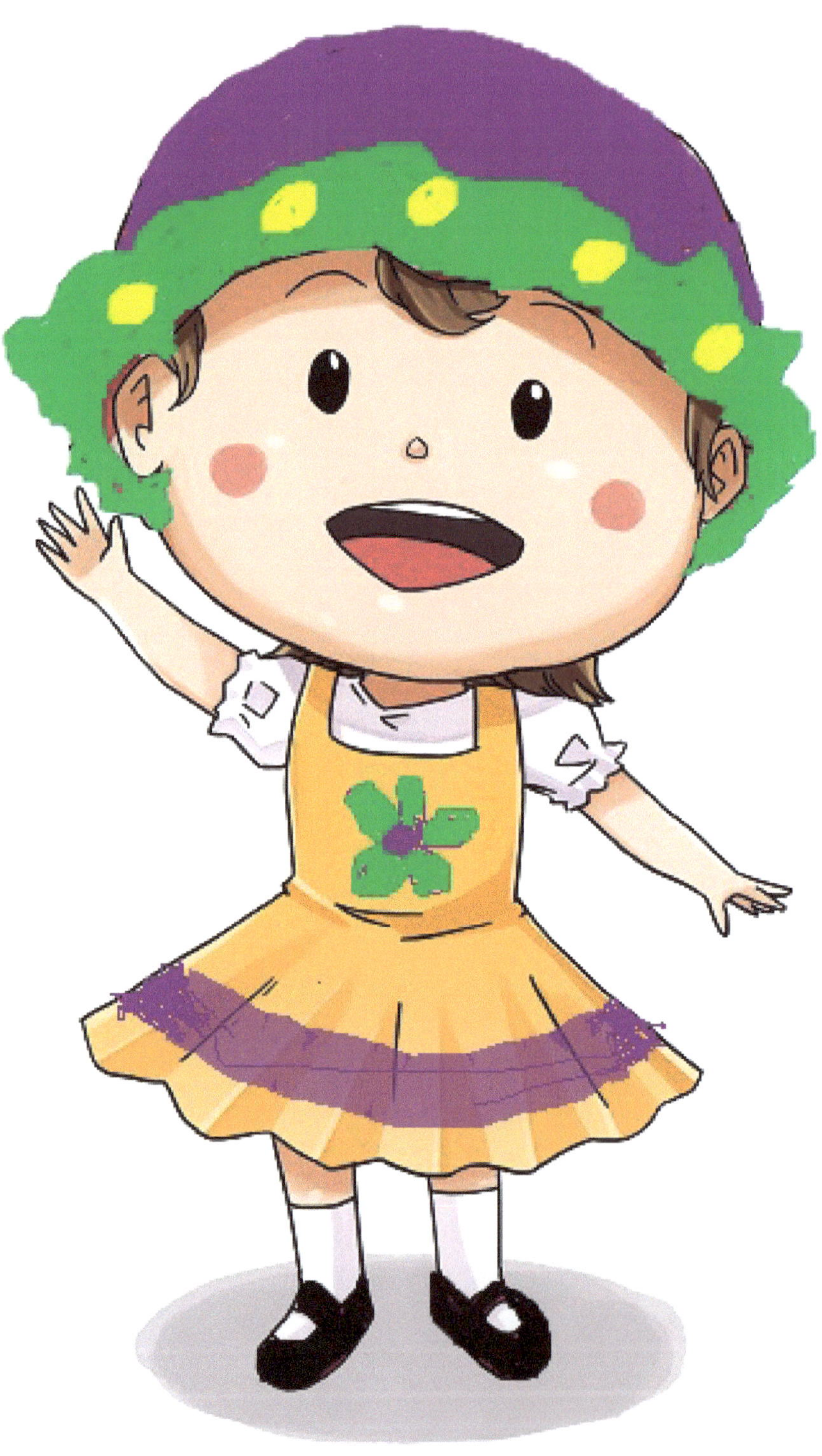

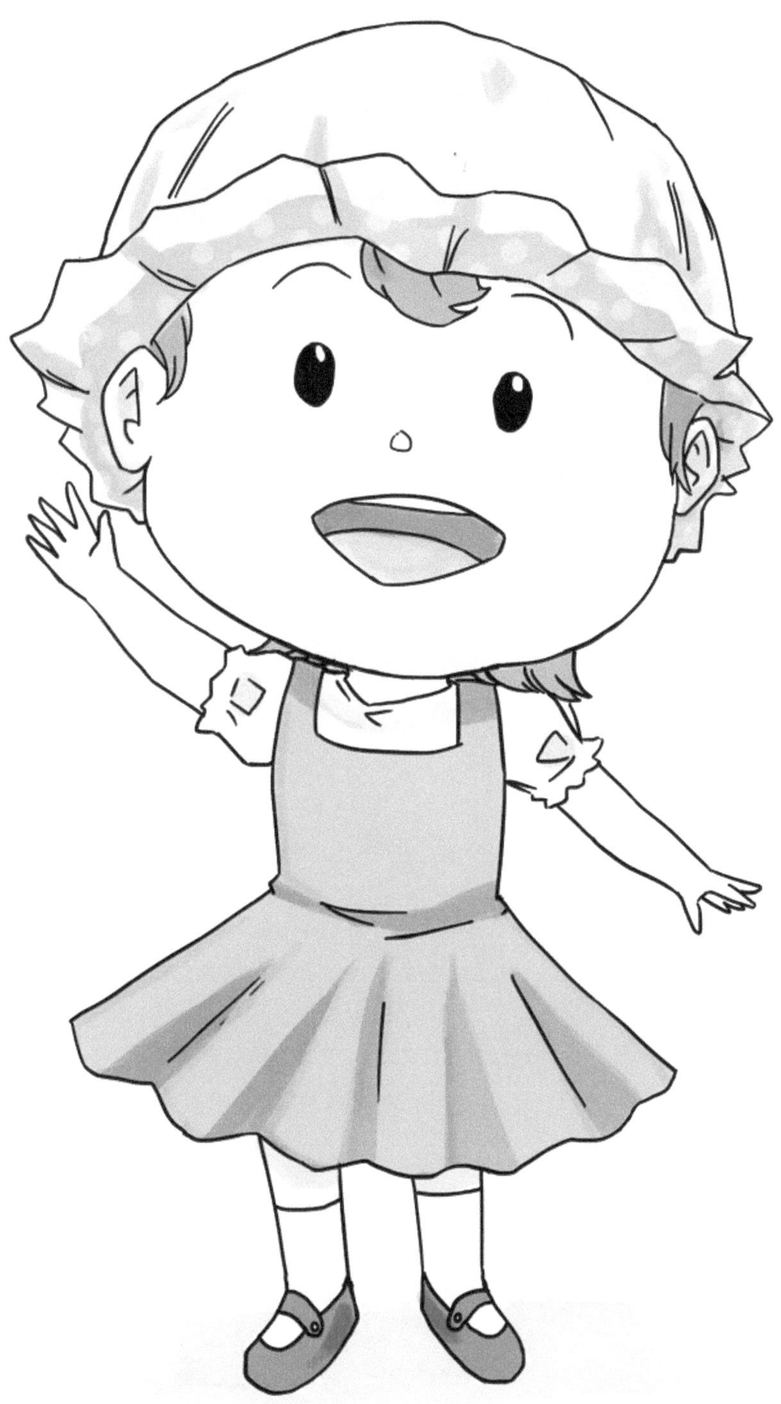

Illustrator Corina Alvarez Loeblich

corina.alvarez.loeblich

Designer Karina Bergstrom

children_blob_publishing

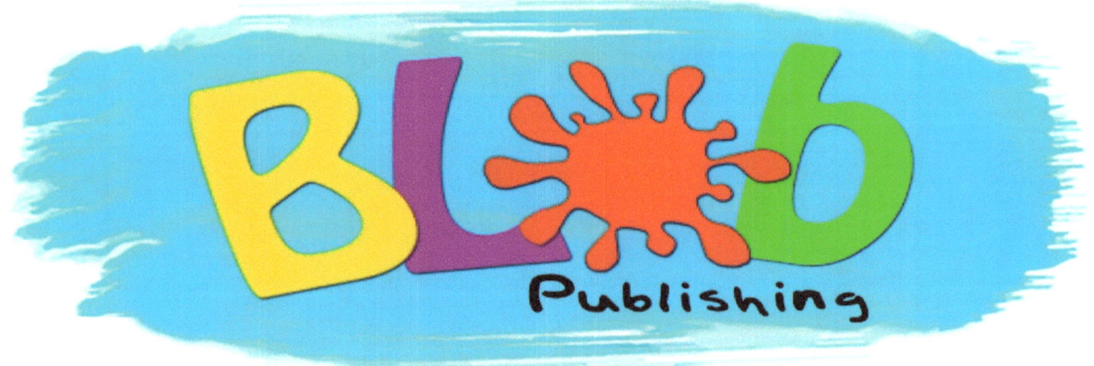